Contents

Words in bold, **like this**, are explained in the Glossary.

Why do animals have ears?

People have ears, and so do many animals. We use our ears to listen to all sorts of sounds. Listen. Can you hear any sounds? Hearing helps you to be aware of the world around you.

Animal ears are different shapes and sizes. Some rabbits have long, floppy ears. Rabbits' ears look quite different to your ears.

Outer ears

Many animals have ears that are easy to see. The outer parts stick out. A donkey's **outer ears** collect sounds. The sounds then go into the donkey's **ear holes**.

Birds have no outer ears. They only have ear holes. This vulture has one hole on each side of its head. Sounds go into the holes so the bird can hear them.

Pointed ears

The lynx has pointed ears, shaped like **triangles**. Tufts of hair grow from the tips. The tufts help the lynx to hear when it is hunting in the long grass.

Aardvarks' ears are long and pointed to help them hear. These animals are **nocturnal**. They spend the night hunting for **insects** to eat. They can hear the sounds of insects called **termites** in a nest.

Rounded ears

The slow loris has rounded ears, shaped like little shells. Its ears gather sounds from the forest. The slow loris uses its **sense** of hearing and of smell to search for birds and **insects** to eat.

Mice use their rounded ears to hear each other's squeaks. Baby mice squeak to their mother. The mother mouse listens to make sure they are safe.

Big ears

Elephants in Africa have the biggest ears of any **mammal**. They use them to listen to the calls of other elephants. They flap their ears to keep cool, too.

At night, foxes use their ears to hunt for food in the dark. A bat-eared fox has big, **sensitive** ears. Its sharp hearing helps it to find **insects** to eat.

Small ears

Sea lions live and hunt in the sea. They have tiny ears. These do not stick out and slow them down when they swim. You can just see their small **outer ears**.

A hippopotamus has tiny ears that it can close. To keep cool, hippos spend lots of time in rivers and lakes. They close their ears to stop the water getting in.

Hidden ears

Birds' ears are often hidden under their feathers. They only have an **ear hole** on each side of their head. Birds listen to each other's songs and calls.

Some animals' ears are completely hidden.
A snake does not have ear holes. As a
snake cannot hear very well, it relies on
other **senses** such as sight and smell.

Ears on top

Many animals have ears on the top of their head. When zebras are busy drinking or **grazing**, their ears help them listen for danger. If they hear a **predator** coming, they quickly run away.

A hare has tall ears on the top of its head.
It sits very still with its tall ears sticking up
above the grass. It listens out for predators,
such as a fox.

Ears at the sides

Monkeys and apes have ears at the sides of their head. Howler monkeys often listen to each other calling. They shout to other **troops** so that they keep away.

African buffalo have ears that stick out at the sides. Huge curved horns stand out above their ears. If a buffalo hears a lion, it may chase it away with its sharp horns.

Moving ears

Many animals raise their **outer ears** when they are listening carefully. It helps them hear better. Sheep dogs do this when they listen to orders from the **shepherd**.

Many animals, such as kangaroos, can turn each ear in a different direction. By doing this, they can work out where a sound is coming from.

Ears in the dark

Many **nocturnal** animals use their ears to help find their **prey** in the dark. The long-eared bat's ears help it to find moths to eat. It also listens for **echoes** to find its way.

Kiwis are nocturnal birds that cannot fly.
They cannot see each other in the long
undergrowth, so they use their ears to listen
out for each other's calls.

Underwater ears

You cannot see fishes' ears. They are hidden inside their heads. They can hear well through the water. Catfish have very good hearing. They can even hear noises made on the shore.

Trout hear very well. Some trout swim off when they hear someone getting into the water. If they hear a **predator**, they swim away to safety.

Ears on legs!

Insects have their ears in unusual places. Crickets have ears on their front legs. They use them to hear and find other crickets in the undergrowth.

Instead of ears, a spider uses hairs to pick up sounds. Rows of special hairs on its legs pick up **vibrations**. These tell the spider if a moving animal is large or small. If it is large, the spider might hide.

Fact file

● Dogs' ears can hear sounds that people cannot hear. They can hear very high sounds, like the sounds of a whistle.

● A bird can hear the sound of its own chick, even amongst a large flock of other singing birds and chicks.

● Crocodiles have ears on top of their head. They can lie in the water with their ears sticking out. This means they can hear while hiding.

Eastern grey kangaroos have a good sense of hearing.

Glossary

ear hole   part of an ear that sound travels into

echoes   sounds, such as a shout, that come back through the air

grazing   eating low-growing grass and plants

insect   small animal with three main parts to its body, and six legs

mammal   animal that feeds its babies with the mother's milk. People are mammals.

nocturnal   awake and active at night, not during the day

outer ear   the part of an ear that sticks out from the head

predator   animal that hunts other animals for food

prey   animals hunted as food

sense   way of being aware of the world (seeing, hearing, smelling, touching and tasting are senses)

sensitive   pick up sounds easily

shepherd   person who looks after sheep

triangle   shape with three corners

troop   group of monkeys

vibrations   tiny movements, made by sounds

Index